Constelldriftongue

Mark Cunningham

Constelldriftongue
© 2023 by Mark Cunningham
All rights reserved.
Published by Mark Cunningham
ISBN 979-8-9882957-2-3

Thanks to Linda Kobert, Christopher Simmons, harry k stammer, Amy Stephenson, and Mark Young.

Among its other aspects, this book is an homage to *Burnham's Celestial Handbook* by Robert Burnham, Jr. Most unacknowledged quotations herein are from the *Handbook*, which forms the warp and weft of this book.

Table of Contents

Sagittarius Milky Way	1
Sagittarius	2
Cygnus	18
Pegasus	24
Sculptor	32
Andromeda	33
Aries	47
Orion	53
Gemini	76
Serpens Caput	85
Norma	93
Ophiuchus	94
Scorpius	103
Serpens Cauda	104
Lyra	110

Constelldriftongue

SAGITTARIUS MILKY WAY

ECHO

not a leak

WIDE NETS OF HEAVEN

and a "long bandage"
in case you miss

THE USUAL SITUATION

observers in

SAGITTARIUS

ARTIST

I can draw
a bow

NICE PANTS

Arrow

YOU MUST BE ONE WITH
THE TARGET, OR SOMETHING

Aratus spoke of the Bow
and the Archer
as though they were
separate constellations

PRODUCT PLACEMENT

or you must become one
with Target

CHARLIE DON'T SURF

Eratosthenes said centaurs
don't use bows

DON'T

you'll shoot your eye out

REMEMBER

the Hathaway man?

BEAUTIFUL MUSIC
TOGETHER

she gives Woody Allen
a harmonica
so he can develop
that side of himself

THIRD DATE

the exchange of material
may be affecting
the normal pattern
of evolution
of both components

EXPLAINS THE
CONFUSION

of Sumerian
origin

TIP OF THE ARROW

so of course
it has
an alternate
name

HOOFS/HOOVES

I wished I called
the book *71 Leafs*

I WAS IN TORONTO ONCE

I mean,
it's Maple *Leafs*

TROLL

I really like the movie
Troll Hunter,
but I guess it doesn't
have a lot to do with centaurs

HUNTER

was Tab cola
named after
Tab Hunter?

INSIDE/OUTSIDE

"The Point"
"The Junction"

HALF EMPTY, HALF FULL

either way,
give it your all

GLARY

impressive, but not
much of an impression,
or a big impression,
but not very impressive

X-RAY ENERGY

you don't need a pair
of those special
x-ray glasses
to see through space
unless it's really glary

ANOTHER WAY I'M NOT
LIKE JAMES ELLROY

I never ordered
the X-ray glasses
advertised in comic books

A VERY SMALL AND DENSE GALACTIC TYPE

it's been decades
since I've seen kids
playing jacks

A DENSE GALACTIC TYPE

I could make it
to eights or maybe
nines, but after that
I wasn't fast enough

ZERO IS NOT NOTHING

I count on it
and from it

NO WONDER I CAN'T LOSE WEIGHT

"mass is not an intrinsic
property of a body
but it is in fact
a reflection of
the whole of the universe
in that body"
(Henri Bortoft, *The Wholeness of
    Nature* 5-6)

IRREDUCIBILITY OF THE
WHOLE

"Southern Segment
of the Bow"
or "The Southern Bow"

OF COURSE IT DOES

the star Beta Lyrae itself
presents the same
constellation
of problems

THE STAR OF THE
PROCLAMATION
OF THE SEA (I)

I'm out of breath already

THE STAR OF THE
PROCLAMATION
OF THE SEA (II)

all stars spit
when they
give out
information

DADDY-O

W. Bidelman in 1954
classified the system
as "*Ape*"

EXPLAIN THE CONFUSION

there was a gorilla
(I think it was a gorilla)
at the St. Louis Zoo
that would spit at
people who made fun of it

WELL ON ITS WAY

to another
minimum

THE BULB CAME ON OVER MY
HEAD, BUT

"the light curve
goes in
the wrong direction"

AN OVERABUNCANCE
OF CARBON

a committee meeting

EVERYTHING IN THE WORLD

either one thing
or another;
either this or that;
either before or after

UNUSUAL VARIABLE

looks
pretty normal

SUDDENLY BEGINS TO FADE

we didn't notice
at first

PSEUDO

when you say
the word
the "p"
isn't really there

AND/BOTH NOT AND/OR

it's not a very
convincing duck
and it's not a very
convincing rabbit

ONE OF THOSE DAYS

completely unobservable
while the sun
is passing through

ROLE OF METAPHOR

like
the more transparent

OVAL VANCANCIES

empty
is already not
nothing

DARK

not completely "dark"

"DARK"

not completely dark

CATALOGUE OF 182 DARK MARKINGS IN THE SKY

if only
I could write that book

A CHART OF NEW STARS
IN THE EARLIEST STAGES
OF FORMATION

little black dots

MUST BE VERY FAINT

peppered with
countless faint
star images

AN EARLY DESCRIPTION

"a nebula
which has never
been discovered"

SWAN/HORSESHOE

looks like
a duck

TRAIN OF LIGHT

swan,
horseshoe,
the perfect form or a ray
or tail of a comet,

a spindle,
a curved hook,
a ghostly figure 2

A PHENOMENON CANNOT
BE SEPARATED FROM
THE INSTRUMENT USED
TO MEASURE IT

"this star system appears
as a double
in small telescopes,
and as a multiple system
in larger ones"

NOT EVEN 10 POUNDS HEAVIER

it looks for all the world
like a huge illuminated
transparency, the dark
rifts appearing just
as they do on photographs

DARK RIFTS

every punk band
should have done a cover
of Black Sabbath's "Paranoid"

"BRIGHT RIM" FEATURES

any feature
is a bright rim

SOMETHING OF A PUZZLE

most people I know
like crossword puzzles,
but I don't

DON'T LIKE IT

and to hell with Sudoku

A SLOW DAY

about 7,500 star images
were counted on a plate

ANONG THE SIXTH FINEST

it's the sixth finest

RESOLVE

probably ranks;
distinctly;
there can be no doubt;
definitely; now thought
to be serious over-estimates

RE-OBSERVE (I)

discovered in 1746,
re-observed in 1764—
better check
those dates again

RE-OBSERVE (II)

that *is* Ramsay

THAT TIRELESS OBSERVER

if I have my glasses on,
my eyes keep trying
to focus even
if they're closed

LIKE EVERYTHING ELSE

apparently floating
in a blank vacancy

NOT ESPECIALLY RICH AGGREGATION

I didn't have any
pennies when I
left the house,
but now I have four

VARIABLE 17

the inability to remember
all of the first 16

VARIABLE 18

can't tell which of
the 16 I've forgotten

LAGOON

sometimes I don't remember
whether the episode
of *Gilligan's Island*
was in color

SIMMER DOWN

16 variables reported
in 1902;
from then to
1973, another 16

SLOW DOWN

send tar

VARIABLE 19

most days
I'd pick
Mary Ann

SAG

the older I get
the more I notice
the "Sag"
in "Sagittarius"

A LITTLE NEBULOUS PATCH (I)

you (meaning: I) would think
it would be "Saggitarius"

A LITTLE NEBULOUS PATCH (II)

twenty-six minutes ago

NEUTRAL CARBON

you rarely remember
the person reading
the newspaper
four seats
in front of you
on the subway

LIKE EVERYTHING ELSE

apparently floating
in a blank vacancy

A REFRESHING VIEW

equals 90 suns

CYGNUS

A SUPER IMPOSE

a superimposed circle
smaller than a dust grain,
but weighing
billions of tons

A DIFFICULT OBJECT

in itself in
the field

THE OLD SHELL GAME (I)

Helen and Castor and Polydeuces
from one egg;
Castor and Polydeuces
from one egg,
Helen and Clytemnestra
from another;
Polydeuces and Helen
are children of Zeus,
Castor and Clytemnestra
are children of Tyndareus,
King of Sparta

THE OLD SHELL GAME (II)

Zeus, Tyndar*eus*

THE OLD SHELL GAME (III)

how many are Polydeuces?

WHAT JUNG NEVER SAID
ABOUT ARCHTYPES

stop me
if you've heard
this one before

AN ARGUMENT

outbursts probably
originate in the redder
component

ACCRETED MATTER

fast food cola cups
on the floor of
the back seat; Kleenex
under couch cushions;
pennies; extension
cords jumbled up

GOOD FOR THE VEIL NEBULA

"no doubt the Veil
is expanding into
a dusty region
and sweeping up
the inter-stellar material
as it does so"

WE HAVE IT ALL

Deneb in the tail
has an actual luminosity
of about 60,000 suns;
the Veil Nebula,
"long and shelving
undulations of a thin
cataract of light, as it
slips from star to
star in its shining fall
through space";
Cygnus X-1,
a black hole in the middle
of the Swan's neck
(Kelvin McKready
quoted by Burham 805)

BLACK HOLE

and you ain't seen nothing yet

ALBIREO

"It started with an Arabic
translation of the Greek
for 'bird,' *ornis*, the name
by which both Aratus
and Ptolemy knew
the constellation. In
the Middle Ages
this Arabic name was
mistranslated back into Latin,
where it was described
as *ab ireo*,
meaning that it was thought
to come from the name
of a certain herb. This phrase
was itself mistaken for
an Arabic name
and was rewritten as *albireo*,"
which is completely
meaningless
(Ian Ridpath, *Star Tales* 60-
61)

MISSING

Carlo Rovelli says
a black hole
is missing information

PTOLEMY

you don't pronounce the "p"

JUNG

It's fun to irritate people
by pronouncing the "j"

ONE PIECE OF INFORMATION
THE BLACK HOLE IS MISSING

the image was subsequently found
on a plate taken
in Copenhagen
on August 16, 1920

MAYBE ORIGINS ARE
RECOVERABLE AFTER ALL

modern drawings have the Swan
in full flight, but
old drawings have the Swan
just lifting off from the ground

LOW-POWER FIELDS

I wonder why
more things
don't just explode

THE HAMMER, THE FEATHER

falling at the same
rate is not failing
at the same rate

YOU HAVE TO LEARN HOW TO PLAY THE SILENCE

Etc.;
trimming the hair
on the outside
of my ear; a term
meaning "a large
air bubble
under the brittle
ice of a puddle"

GLORIOUS SIGHTS

dandelion fluff
adrift in no
breeze; spider
silk unspooling;
as you sleep your
eyes still move.

STARTING OVER (I)

black holes
evaporate

STARTING OVER (II)

1 Days

PEGASUS

THE GREAT SQUARE

most astronomers
are a little uncool

SCARS OF PUBERTY

negative numbers
mean *brighter*

"SPRINGS OF THE OCEAN"

there must be a lot of them
to make the ocean
wobble so much

MANY OTHER FABULOUS ADVENTURES

since that time
I ended up
with sugar all over
the back seat,
I use two plastic
bags when I
get bulk sugar—
and I get
a paper sack
at checkout, too

NOT SUPPORTED
BY ANCIENT MYTHS

Pop-Tarts

SUPPORTED
BY MODERN SCIENCE

the box says the Pop-Tarts
are "Produced with
Genetic Engineering"

WEAK EMISSION
FEATURES (I)

not accurately known;
uncertain;
seems reasonable

WEAK EMISSION
FEATURES (II)

I hope the Pop-Tarts
aren't produced with very
much genetic engineering

REQUIRES NO
TRANSLATION

only if you
already know
what it means

COMING AND GOING

most constellations are
at the same time

BREATH, ANYWAY

The Nose, or The Mouth

WELL, DUH

"the apparent pendulum-
like oscillation of a small star
in the same vertical
as the large one,
when the telescope
is swung from side to side"

AND THEN

the fine globular star
cluster M15 may be
found in binoculars
by sweeping
an area about 4 degrees
to the northwest

GROUCHO

so *that's*
how it got
in my binoculars

NO REAL CONNECTION

always say that
just before you
make a connection

CLOSE TO ACTUAL CONTACT

sorry

ONE OF THE MOST INTERESTING OF BINARY SYSTEMS

does anybody remember
Elizabeth Taylor
and Richard Burton?

REMEMBER SWEATER GIRLS?

a very fine
specimen of
a completely
insulated system

LICK OBSERVATORY

if only

ECCENTRICITY

I always brush
my left teeth first

FRUSTRATINLY DIFFICULT

26.27 years

YALE CATALOGUE OF BRIGHT
STARS

I bet they think
they have a lot of them

A SERIES OF OBSERVATIONS

visual range differs
from photographic
range, but
you perceive
a photograph visually

A CLARIFICATION

8 hr. 59 min. 41 s.
or just a few seconds short of 9
        hours

SLOWLY DECREASING SINCE DISCOVERY

according to information
theory, information is
physical, so when you
look at something
you drain some of
information,
and when its information
is drained completely,
it ceases to exist: so
we should ban
stare-down matches
among grade schoolers

IF YOU DIDN'T UNDERSTAND THAT

don't read it again

AN INTERESTING PROBLEM

any light I see
is already dated
by the time
I see it

ENQUIRING MINDS WANT TO KNOW (I)

but by who?

ENQUIRING MINDS WANT TO KNOW (II)

or should that be "by whom?"

THE ORIGINAL SPECTRUM WAS OF TYPE BE

only after looking at it
for a few seconds
did I realize
the copperhead was dead

NEBULOSITY IS DIRECTELY OBSERVABLE

well, I think
that's what that is

AGAINST HUMILITY

modest telescopes
achieve only
partial resolution

FAINT TIDAL STREAMERS

sometimes I think that
describes the blood
in my capillaries

SCATTERED IN THE INDIVIDUAL

sometimes I think *that*
describes the blood
in my capillaries

SCULPTOR

BEFORE THE SURGERY

scared

AFTER THE SURGERY

scarred

ANDROMEDA

MISFORTUNES

began one day

PREDICTABLE

a female character
will be the one
who survives the horror film

MARILYN BURNS

even if she can't
run very well
and the other actors
really don't like her

STAND AND DELIVER

not the motto
of any logistics
company I know

ALPHA AND OMEGA (I)

Adam Ant
to
Atom Ant

ALPHA AND OMEGA (II)

Atom Ant
to
Adam Ant

THAT WAS THEN, THIS IS NOW

andro-media?

INTRODUCTION TO THE UNIVERSE

who or what
would you
introduce it to?

REPRESENT

let these squiggly lines here
represent those
squiggly lines over there

ALPHA

manganese

LIGHT TIME LAG

sometimes called
"Sirrah"

800 TIMES FAINTER THAN
THE SUN

still, you don't
want it shining
right in your eyes

SUSPECTED OF SLIGHT
VARIABILITY

now and then

DEFINITE

greenish-blue

99.9% OF THE UNIVERSE

slightly displaced from
the position of
sharpest focus

WIDE COMMON MOTION

there must be
something on
the sidewalk
up there

ARE THEY DATING?

interesting to
compute the probable
actual separation

VERY SMALL PARTIAL ECLIPSES

you know
what I mean

ABSORPTION LINES

somebody's been sunbathing

WATCH THE SKIES

Harvard patrol plate

ADDED COMPLICATION (I)

the exact
figure depends

ADDED COMPLICATION (II)

Denise,
not demise

ADDED COMPLICATION (III)

omega is double

COUNTLESS

224

MAY BE FOUND IN
ALMOST ANY PART
OF THE CITY

the sky

IN THE SAME FIELD

different grasses

DEFINITE

definite
relation change

FROM OBSERVATIONS
AT HARVARD

ups
and downs

A NORMAL MINIMUM

the glass is empty

THE SPECTRUM IS COMPOSITE

two eyes
and a blink

TYPICAL

perhaps
the *most*
typical

FASCINATING UNCERTAINTIES

what *are* these
leftovers in
the Tupperware containers

AN APPARENTLY
CONTINUOUS
BACKGROUND (I)

you don't even
notice it

AN APPARENTLY CONTINUOUS BACKGROUND (II)

you're a big kid
when you realize
the background
of cartoons repeats:
Daffy has passed
that tree three times

THE BACKGROUND OF CARTOONS REPEATS

imagine
giving directions

AN APPARENTLY CONTINUOUS BACKGROUND (III)

I've always liked the Droopy
cartoon where Droopy
and the Wolf miss
a turn and run over
the edge of the film
into white space

BLACK SPACE

will anyone put out
classic Hollywood films
in their actual ratio?

ALL HAIL

chief object

CHIEF

I remember
The Beverly Hillbillies'
joke about Chief Meteorologist

A PERSIAN ASTRONOMER

Al Sufi

A NAME I WISH I HAD

A. H. Joy

A DEFINITE, OBVIOUS
NAKED-EYE OBJECT

a small, elongated
bit of
fuzzy light

MOST THINGS ARE EVENTUALLY

"actually it is
round and flat"

ROUND AND FLAT

it is not expected
that any further
great revision
will be required

A MULTITUDE OF
INDIVIDUAL STARS

I'll still take Fred Astaire
and Ginger Rogers

A MULTITUDE OF
INVIDUAL LESS-THAN-
STARS

Juan Ramon Jimenez
once wondered
if he was seeing the moon
or just an advertisement
for the moon: now
I wonder if I'm seeing
the moon or just
a computer-generated
special effect

CUBIC LIGHT YEARS

but light bulbs
are round or
spiral or tear drop
or tubes

WHEN YOU LEAST EXPECT IT

the hum
of power lines

KARAOKE

I like to make
Merzbow noises
in the shower

THE DUST IN INDUSTRIAL

"industrial music"
is really nostalgic

AT ANY MOMENT ANYWHERE

found to be
surrounded by
some 140 objects

DO SPIRAL ARMS LEAD
OR TRAIL

they trail

WHEN CORRECTED FOR
DISTANCE

things are brighter

APPLIES TO NOW, TOO,
SO. . . .

of course its actual
significance was not
realized at the time

BUT IN SPACE, NO ONE
CAN HEAR YOUR FILLINGS

every normal galaxy
is at least a weak
transmitter of
radio radiation

OPEN UNIVERSE

all four of these
small systems are open
for observation

DEAR NSA

like NCG 752
I make my best
impression in
a relatively small
rich-field instrument
with wide-angle eye pieces

THE SO-CALLED
"FORBIDDEN LINES"

I can't tell you
what was supposed
to go here

AS ALWAYS

the brightest was found
to be a non-member

MAY YET BE FOUND

the screw driver with
the yellow handle;
the John Zorn CD
I can't remember
the name of; a
good snow shovel

POPULATION APPEARS TO END
RATHER ABRUPTLY

wait till a new
Wal-Mart opens

~~AMATUER~~ AMATEUR

I have to take off
my glasses before
I do my stretches

C. R. O'DELL POINTS OUT

the apparent brightness
of a star surrounded
by strong nebulosity
is critically correlated
with the seeing

SUPERFICIAL LIKENESS

I sort of like her
because she sort of
looks like someone
I once sort of knew

BINARY

96.69

MATHEMATICAL UNCONSCIOUS

96.69

AS ABOVE, SO BELOW

but never at the same time:
as Carlo Rovelli writes,
"every object in the universe
has its own time, running
at a pace determined by
the local gravitational field,"

and at the Planck scale
Quantum events are "no longer
ordered by the passage of time"
(*Reality is Not What It Seems* 178)

GRAVITY

or, as Charles Wright has it,
"an inch of music is an inch and a
      half of dust"

CLOSED

the light is beautiful
when I close my eyes

ANOTHER VIEW

it could be
the result of
an exceptionally
lazy nova

I'M NOT TALKING IN MY SLEEP

that's the television
in the next room

ARIES

RAM

8.5 miles
per second
in approach

MAYBE WAIT A MINUTE

King Athamas of Boeotia
was about to sacrifice
his son Phrixus
to ward off an *impending*
famine

BAD NEWS (I)

and the message from
the oracle
was a fake

BAD NEWS (II)

Phrixus:
a bad name
to have in junior high

IT'S NOT A HORSE, SO LOOK IT IN THE MOUTH

In thanks, Phrixus sacrificed
the winged, golden ram
Nephele sent to save him

WHAT DID YOU THINK IT WOULD DO?

after his death, Phrixus's
ghost returned
to haunt

SPIRITS

I worked for a year in a hotel
that had been the old city
hospital, and the laundry room
had been the city morgue,
and if there were any spirits
in there we got along just fine

I HEAR VOICES

I wish I had the kind of voice
that would be good
for car commercials

MYTH

but I don't watch (check
another game) or listen
(mute button) to commercials

UNCANNY

it's always odd to see
"in real life"
a person you normally
see only on TV
or hear on the radio

COARSE SPIRAL

I'll turn around
to look at someone
I find interesting

GOLDEN FLEECE

Cambridge University Press
can't expect to sell
many books if it's
going to price thin hardbacks
at $75-125—just to
libraries and specialists
who have to have
the information at hand

NOTHING NEW

Jack Kerouac, 1952:
"the latest sounds in
hip bop are exactly
like the latest developments
in N. Y. Advertising"
(*Book of Sketches* 180)

ACCORDING TO INFORMATION
THEORY

you don't own information:
you are it
and you give it away:
your hand *is* information

FOOTNOTE

I'm just
a footnote
to a long history
of DNA sequencing

OR

a place-holder,
a link

OR

or DNA*s*,
since mitochondria,
at least, have
their own DNA

A DILEMMA

Sharatan, from the Arabic
meaning "two" of something
(possibly two signs
or two horns, for it was
originally applied both
to this star
and to its neighbor,
Gamma Arietis)

A CURIOUSLY CORRUPT
FORM OF AL-SARATAN

Mesarthim

PLACE-HOLDER
SEQUENCE

when I say "my ego"
who or what is the "my"?

PLACE-HOLDER

in Greek times, Aries
contained the point of
the vernal equinox,
where the Sun
crosses the celestial
equator from north to south

PLACE-HOLDER, SEQUENCE (I)

Molly Hatchet
is still together, only
now the group
is playing at
the local casino

PLACE-HOLDER, SEQUENCE (II)

my hair used to have
a natural part
in the middle: now
the natural part
is a little bit to the left

IN SEQUENCE

because of precession,
the vernal equinox has moved
30 degrees and lies
in the constellation Pisces

ORION

SMALL RANGE

5 million miles
from the center
of gravity

CULMINATING IN SOMETHING CLOSE TO SPLENDOR

I always put a little Splenda
in my Americano

NATURALLY BECOMES VISIBLE (I)

but I wear glasses

NATURALLY BECOMES VISIBLE (II)

the problem with contact
lenses is the contact:
I don't like
anything near to my eyes

MIDNIGHT CULMINATION

that's so yesterday

VISIBLE FROM EVERY
INHABITED PART OF THE EARTH

the Armpit
of the Giant

NO MAN IS A HERO
TO HIS VALET

"originally did not refer
to a 'giant'
but was a term used
for a sheep marked with
a central spot or belt"

THE GREAT ONE HAS FALLEN

time for a commercial

BROUGHT TO YOU BY

the "Amazon star"

AMAZON STAR

brought to you: buy

LIKE EVERYTHING ELSE

and, anyway, the Sumerians
had already made
the constellation:
Orion was Gilgamesh
fighting the Bull of Heaven

WARM WEATHER

I always spell "Sumerian"
"Summerian"

A SINGLE MISTY STAR TO THE EYE AIDED BY TENNYSON

"a single misty star"
(Tennyson)

"'a single misty star'
to the unaided eye"
(Burnham)

NOT VISIBLE FROM EVERY INHABITED PART OF THE EARTH

but if you went to
the uninhabited part
to check, it would
no longer be uninhabited

ERRATIC

earratic

BUT MY FEET ARE LONGFELLERS

masses
of luminous gasses

AND

using "&"
doesn't make it
more intense

HEGEL

Betelgeuse,
Betelgeux,
Beetlejuice

AUTHORITARIAN

if they don't have
a sense of humor about themselves,
they're probably authoritarians

AUTHOR

trust me,
I know

THE EXOTIC WORD IS FUN
TO TYPE, TOO

padparadaschah

THERE'S ALWAYS
SOMEBODY

"or deep topaz"

MAYBE AN OUTRIGHT
ERROR

still, say it
with emphasis
on "right"

LEARN FROM THE BEST

"as he faced
the rising sun
his sight
was returned"

ACCORDING TO LEVINAS

light, like ontology,
totality, ego, and discourse,
is a source of
the State and violence,
but night risks a worse
violence, since it lacks even
the possibility of communication—so
maybe a star or constellation
is a good image for, well,
something good, since a star
or constellation is neither darkness
nor totalizing light: 10,000 years ago
a constellation did not look the way
it looks today, and 10,000 years
        from now
it will not look the way it does today:
what we see now is only
a connect-the-dots sketch
on our part—but then we try to
turn it into a figure of the Same,
rather than realizing or respecting
that it is never fully knowable (and
we're behind, since light takes
        thousands
or even millions of years to reach
        us,
and the star or constellation may not
even be there now) (whenever
now is): but, then again, we
can never really be sure an object

or person is *not* fully known,
because there's no way to
tell: "infinitely unknowable"
means we never know
for sure one way or the other:
we are always only
approaching, but never
reaching, any certainty

FIELD STARS

in the photograph
of 10-year-olds
at a picnic table
at a birthday party,
I can't tell which one is me

OBSERVATION BY LOW
POWER

the way that can be
spoken of is not
the eternal way,
and the name
that can be named
is not the eternal name,
and . . . you get the drift

MOVING ON

Pindar calls the constellation *Oarion*

TO MAKE GIBBER:
FOR H. P. LOVECRAFT

an Arabian name, "Al Babadur,"
the Strong One;
a better-known Arabian name,
"Al Jabbar," the Giant;
the Syriac "Gabbara,"
the Jewish, "Gibbor"

NO ABDUL-JABBAR

I can name
Jerry West,
Gail Goodrich,
Elgin Baylor,
and Wilt Chamberlain
from the 1971-1972
Los Angeles Lakers team
that won 33 straight games,
but I usually forget
Happy Hairston,
the forward other than Baylor,
and—blast it—Jim McMillan,
who replaced Baylor, who retired
9 games into the season

UNDEFEATED

I haven't lost at
tic-tac-toe
for over 25 years

NOT THE GREAT HUNTER

Wilt preferred the nickname
The Big Dipper, given to him
by friends who saw him
dip his head
to go through doorways

INTERACTIVE PICTURE
PROCESSING SYSTEM

"are evidently true features
on the star;
they represent. . . ."

ALMOST PROPHETIC
VISION

maybe if I squint

REPAYS LONG
OBSERVATION

to make fame
nothing

7th BRIGHTEST STAR

John, Paul, George, Ringo,
Brian Epstein, Pete Best:
so Jimmie Nicol, who replaced
Ringo for concerts in Denmark
and Japan in 1964 (Ringo
had tonsillitis), would be the 7th

TO MAKE FAME NOTHING

Jimmie went bankrupt
in 1965

ALWAYS NOTICE THE NEXT WORD

the breaking up of a mackerel
sky

IN SPACE NO ONE CAN HEAR YOU LAUGH

"solemn depths of space"

THE EARTH'S ATMOSPHERE

incurable
unsteadinesss

A GOOD TYPO

"unsteadinesss"

BREATHING

curable
unsteadiness

VITURALLY OBSOLETE

these days,
this means
really obsolete

IN PROGRESS AT THE
PRESENT TIME

the present

THERE'S A FUZZY LINE

between diffuse
nebulosity and
regular nebulosity

SOMETHING LIKE 57,000
TIMES

I've spelled de Kooning
"de Koonig"

AMERICA ♥ ORION

the Belt, the
Girdle,
moving farther out

0.00000002

I'm leaning toward pizza

EXCITED TO LUMINOSITY

I *do* remember
The Leaning Tower of Pizza

GREAT INTENSITY OF HELIUM LINES

so you travel 14,000
light years, meet
some aliens, and your
voice sounds funny

GROSSLY EXAGGERATED

just about anything
exaggerated
becomes gross

OH, WELL

Levinas insists the aliens
wouldn't *really*
understand you, anyway

A CRACK IN THE GROUND
AND A STING IN THE TAIL

besides, as Timothy Morton
points out, "Nature,"
or even "nature,"
is an idea,
a conceptual
reduction of astronomical,
geological, genetic,
and other data
that you (or I)
don't understand fully,
because no one understands
them fully, and because
things reveal only
certain aspects of
themselves—therefore,
any normative
or regulatory system
derived from N/nature
is not as fixed
(well-founded,
accurate) as it's probably
claimed to be
and is,
in fact,
authoritarian

CHART

the "Variations of Betelgeuse—from
Observations of the AAVSO" chart
looks like the map of mouse
droppings on the garage floor

BOTH

I've heard that both slugs
and Styrofoam peanuts
dissolve if sprinkled with water

ONE UNSEEN COMPONENT
IS PRESENT

I've lost a paperclip
on the carpet
and I'm barefoot

NOT ENOUGH TO ROUND UP

"1.00805 day"

ODD VARIABLE

never evens out

EXCEPTIONALLY SLOW

there's *another* new stop light
on the road
around the mall

AT MAXIMUM

you can't really
"casually date"
for more than
two years

20 YEARS OF SCHOOLING AND THEY PUT YOU ON THE DAY SHIFT

still relatively bright
20 years later

I THINK IT'S FUNNY

there's a star named
FU Orionis

AN ODD NOTE

"F peculiar"

X MARKS

those credit card scanners
at the checkout will accept
almost any signature

NO PARTICULAR ORDER

is always some
particular order

DIFFERENT VARIATIONS

possibilities are riches:
I like dimmer switches

5 OR 6 MAGNITUDES
OF OBSCURATION

realism is another name
for the game where
everybody sits in
a circle and passes
a whisper along

SELF-LUMINOUS STATE

burning your finger
doesn't count

THE FINEST EXAMPLE
OF A DIFFUSE NEBULA

that's what they say,
whoever "they" are

IMPRESSIVE BEYOND
WORDS

—pretty cool, huh?
—yeah

THAT'S SWEET

"for the small telescope,
the star has
a bluish companion"

A HARD WORD TO DEFINE
BUT I'M GETTING CLOSER

inchoate

ATE

I always get too much
at those salad bars
that charge by weight,
so it's never inexpensive
like I think it will be

THINGS I LIKE NOW THAT I
DIDN'T USE TO LIKE

banana peppers
egg plant
spinach

STILL DON'T LIKE

green peppers

A FEELING OF AWE AND
SURPISE

a great ghostly bat

A VERY DIFFERENT CLASS OF
OBJECTS

the eyelash in (on)
my eye
is neither me nor not me

"FORBIDDEN RADIATION"

meta-stable
or
me-tast-able?

FOR EXAMPLE

the copyright of the Oxford
edition of Schiller's *On
the Aesthetic Education
of Man* reads
"1967 [i. e. 1968]"

STELLA

what you see is
what *was*
there to see

EARLY DAYS OF
SPECTROSCOPY

a number of
unidentified lines

A HYPOTHETICAL
ELEMENT

does anyone really know
what "teal" is?

IN THE DAYS BEFORE
GRADE INFLATION

the star called "C"

is thus the true
primary of the group

SHOWN

shown in full daylight,
but daylight is shown
in full space as dark

WHY THE NEBULA LOOKS WHITE

50 atoms of chlorine
per cubic foot

NOT SO BIG AFTER ALL

decimal points
omitted to avoid
confusion
with star images

ACCURATE COLORS

I, too, have trouble
telling the difference between
black and navy blue

RESPECT

some portions are approaching

and some receding
with respect
to your position

THE IRREGULAR PATTERN
OF TURBULENCE

the regular pattern
is the universe

FOCUS IS VARIABLE

E. Barnard seems to
have been the first
to recognize it as a great
obscuring mass
of some sort

HOW MUCH NEARER IS
NOT DEFINITELY KNOWN

the spectral type
of the companion

IN OTHER WORDS,
DON'T HOLD YOUR
BREATH

somewhat more uncertain
than the Merope Nebula
in the Pleiades

BAD VACUUM

less than a millionth
the density of
a good laboratory vacuum

A NEGATIVE EVENT

Artemis showed Apollo
what a good shot
she was with her bow
by hitting "a small black object"
floating in the sea,
and then she was grief-stricken
to learn she'd shot Orion,
for whom she was about to give up
her vows of chastity to marry

FLUORESCENT

Mel Bochner
on Dan Flavin, 1967,

no [i. e. 1968] about it
(I don't think so, anyway)

"Up until about fifteen
years ago all light

came as points. All
sources of illumination,

including the sun,
were regulated and radiated

from a point source.
With the proliferation of

fluorescent lighting
a perceptual revolution

occurred with probably
    deeper
significance than the
    invention

of light bulbs (which
still created chiaroscuro

shadows). Light now
occurs in long straight

lines, obliterating shadows.
It can, in effect, surround"
("Serial Art")

THINK OF THE
HEADACHES

the light
of the Orion Nebula
is largely fluorescent

GEMINI

TWAIN (I)

I never wanted
a brother or sister

TWAIN (II)

I never had
an invisible friend

BUT STILL

always
back up your files

TWICE

he'll make you repeat
everything you say

ABOUT 25 DEGREES FROM THE EDGE-ON POSITION

she said she knew
what she wanted
to say, but not in words

SCANNERS

Scanners II is not nearly
as good as *Scanners*
(no Cronenberg),
but the producers
must have known
people like me
would want to see it

BUT

do they really like me?

AN ENDEARING QUIRK

the phrase
eat eat,
chew chew
always made her
crack up

SUGAR

I used to put two spoonfuls
of sugar in coffee;
now I put only one

VISIBLE FRIEND

the people who put
cream and sugar
in for you
never get it right

JOHN LEE HOOKER

when I saw him
he could still play
half the solos;
somebody else
played the other half

REPEAT

the tendency for blues
singers to repeat
every lyric
gets old fast

DUPLEX

a duplex
has never seemed
a completely desirable
living situation

CLOSE BINARY

I don't want to sit
near couples
who sit on
the same side
of the booth

STILL TOO CLOSE

though located 100
billion miles from
the main pair,
the third star
is still gravitationally
associated with
the rest of the system

SCENE

there is usually one
scene in any movie
that makes me hesitate
to watch the movie
again, because I feel
embarrassed to be watching,
or for the actors, or because
I think the scene
is a misrepresentation of life
and I know I'm supposed
to be moved by it

OVER MY DEAD BODY

always alive when you say that

NOT ONE WITH THE UNIVERSE

when I have a crumb or shred
caught between my teeth,
it bothers me until
I floss its out

CAUGHT

everybody's like that, I guess

MAIL

there was another Mark
        Cunningham
at the university I attended,
and we met once:
he was irritated that he kept getting
my mail, and then he was irritated
even more that I never got his

PHONE

I once talked on the phone
for five minutes to a woman
calling from England before we
realized we didn't know each
        other—

so maybe I got one of
the other Mark Cunningham's
calls, too

REVIEW

once an editor sent me
an email thanking me for
the good review
of his magazine and offering
me a free subscription, but
I had to email him back
and tell him I wasn't
the Mark Cunningham
who'd written the review,
that I didn't write reviews;
I didn't say it struck me
as odd that it didn't strike him
as odd that I'd write
a glowing review right after
he had accepted
some of my pieces
(I guess it really didn't
strike me as odd)

ROLL CALL

there's Robert Bly the poet
and Robert W. Bly, author
of *Bob Bly's Guide to
Freelance Writing Success:
How to Make$100,000
a Year as a Freelance
Writer and Have the Time*

of Your Life; James Tate
the poet and James Tate
the author of children's books;
Charles Wright the poet
and Charles Wright the crime
        novelist;
Robert Grenier the poet
and Robert Grenier the author of
*Basque Shipbuilding and Whaling
in the 16th Century*, and Robert
        Grenier
the author of *88 Days to Kandahar:
a CIA Diary*, and Robert Grenier
the author of *Customer Satisfaction
Though Total Quality Assurance*

TOTAL QUALITY ASSURANCE

I've read that, according
to mathematicians,
you can write a number
at least two ways,
as 9.99 or 10,
for instance, but
this seems
too vague to me

SHED MORE LIGHT

so what if subatomic particles
once in contact
continue to act
as if they were still

in contact after
they have separated:
I still can't find
the damn flashlight

OTHER HALF

there must be some women
writers who have
the other-writers-with-
the-same-name problem, but
I can't think of any

RECOGNIZE

I wonder if I would recognize
a recording of the voice
in my head, if it
could be recorded—but still
I'd be hearing it in my head

PROBABLY NO REAL
CONNECTION

I want a Pez or other
candy dispenser
shaped like a cell phone,
so that when somebody
is talking loudly
on the subway
I can pull out my phone
and talk loudly, too

ONE OF THOSE ILLUISONS

in ultraviolet light,
an Eskimo;
in red light,
a clown

MUST BE THE MORTAL ONE

the skin lotion always
just out of reach
in the middle of the night

MAYBE NOT

I've named some of
the constellations of floaters
in my eyes

BETWEEN

according to occultists,
the power comes from
between the stars

EITHER WAY

the profiles
on the coins
given them
double chins

SERPENS CAPUT

NOT STILL

I always think of
the jagged lines
in Clyfford Still's
paintings as going
down, not up

TAILS, NOT HEADS

"Caput" seems to me
to be the name
of the tail
rather than the head

TURN IT DOWN

both the separation
and the PA
have decreased

DRAWING THE LINE (I)

I've touched a live python
and a rattlesnake skin,
but I won't
touch a worm

DRAWING THE LINE (II)

odd that most people
don't find pasta
a disgusting food

DRAWING THE LINE (III)

I won't eat
vermicelli

ERASING THE LINE

I'm not nearly
as afraid
of blacksnakes
as I used to be

KUNDALINI

this reduction of fear
started about the same time
I learned some yoga stretches

CHOW

I don't think
I could eat
rattlesnake, if
I knew what it was

BUT

as a friend said,
who's to say what's chicken
and what's not

SHOULD BE EXAMINED
WITH LOWEST POWER

maybe a taste

ROE 75

then again, I never thought
I'd like venison

DRAIN

members have been
recruited from virtually
every part
of the sky to be members
of the "Sirius Stream"

OCCASION (I)

naked-eye
visibility

365.75

does not differ significantly
from 357.2

OCCASION (II)

a few weeks
out of each year

LIGHT RANGE

a three-way lamp
is good, but one
setting always burns out
long before the others

VARIATIONS

do not repeat themselves
with absolute regularity

WEALTH

I've always thought the real
measure of wealth
is how many options
you have available to you

INDEFINITE RESOLUTION
(I)

contains no stars,
contains over
half a million

INDEFINITE RESOLUTION
(II)

"the present author first read
Asimov's apocalyptic tale
["Nightfall"] just
two nights after . . . ."

GREAT OBJECT OF
SUMMER

double cheeseburger

A DEFINITE RESOLUTION

I will eat only one
double cheeseburger
a week

I REMEMBER DRIVE INS

projected on a loose,
irregular ground
of stars

OFTEN MENTIONED IN DESCRIPTIONS OF LORD ROSSE

many bright globulars

DOUBLE CHEESEBURGER

maybe I should do some
stretches: I'm starting
to look globular myself

NO TWISTY THOUGHTS

at first, I got to where
I could touch my ankles,
then my feet, and now
I can touch the floor

TWISTY

T. J. Clark on Nicolas Poussin's
drawing titled *A Snake*:
"it is a body that is content
with a constant, and as it were
provisional, intersection
of one bit of itself with another"
(*The Sight of Death* 179)

GRATIFY

"things that gratify you
with new impressions,
that offer you
a million new qualities"
(Francis Ponge,
"Introduction to the Pebble,"
The Power of Language,
tr. Serge Gavronsky 77)

A FACT (I)

since no two double
cheeseburgers
exist in exactly
the same
and are never eaten
at the same time
(and even one is not
eaten at the same time, but
one bite after another,
minutes pass, etc.),
they are different
and the experiences of eating
them are different, too

A FACT (II)

Ponge never wrote about
cheeseburgers, at least
so far as I know:
too American?

SOLID

another phrase from
"Introduction to the Pebble"—
"'lasting' or 'ephemeral,' etc.,
with all the imaginable combinations
of those pitiful qualities"
(*The Power of Language* 77)

A THOUGHT

I'd rather be a lasting ephemeron
than an ephemeral lasting

NORMA

ON THE LEVEL (I)

Norma
is a reassuring name

ON THE LEVEL (II)

I've never known anyone
named Norma

OPHIUCHUS

OFF

Edmund Halley
overthrew the idea
of "fixed stars,"
and now
people pronounce
his name incorrectly

LITTLE CUSS

I remember when I thought
I'd made a new answer
to the "What starts with F
and ends with UCK" joke
by just putting the four letters
together and telling my Mom

DEAR DOCTOR

I wish I'd never read
in the record book
about people who had
the hiccups
for forty years

BUT

but I've always liked
the word "hiccough"

STRAIGHT

do I hold my spine straight
or does it hold me straight

STRAIGHT DOPE

the spine is curved

EINSTEIN

space is curved
and continuous

QUANTUM MECHANICS

space is flat
and discrete

QUANTUM GRAVITY

space is curved (I think)
and discrete

A STEP

thus I defy gravity—
a little—but
I guess it's not
a step if my foot
doesn't come back down

GRAVITY-DEFYING

sounds more impressive

BREAK/BRAKE

"boys by the hundred
plummet through the roof,
quivering and kicking
at the ends of ropes.
The boys hang
at different levels, some
near the ceiling and others
a few inches off the floor"
(William S. Burroughs,
(*Naked Lunch* 167)

WSB

William S. Burroughs credited
his metabolism's having to
recreate itself every time
he got off heroin
for his long life and good health

THE

the "hypo"
in "hypothetical"

S

William S. Burroughs
is often referred to
as William Burroughs,
the S disappearing
according to no criteria
that I can figure out

HOLD ON TO YOURSELF

with what?

REASON AND FASHION
ARE CONCENSUS
OPINIONS

apparent motion
(proper motion)

INTEGRATED
PHOTOGRAPHIC
MAGNITUDE

the Afro-American student
in the crowd
in the photograph

wasn't really at
the football game:
he was air-brushed in later

PLACE

a place for everything
with everything
in a different place

EVEN LIGHT TAKES TIME
TO TRAVEL

rusty orange

THE SKY

bright and easily
located, about
half the time

ABOUT HALF THE TIME

we could call it
the Land of the Noonday Moon,
rather than the
Land of the Midnight Sun

FOR INSTANCE

the most beautiful animal
I've ever seen
was a white and orange
albino python

HIGH FIVES ALL AROUND

this is
a fairly "cool"
star

INCORRUPTIBILITY OF
THE HEAVENS

if you try to bribe it
by tossing a quarter
up to it, the
quarter comes
right back down

INTEREST

scarcely anything shows
through, making this
a picture almost
unequalled in interest

AN OBJECT OF GREAT
INTEREST

spectra obtained
by Joy
at Mt. Wilson

GIGGLES IN HEALTH CLASS

an interesting pair,
presenting a fine
study in
structural contrast

THE BIG O

Oscar Robertson
probably wouldn't
have the same
nickname today

A TWIST IN THE TAIL

or would he?

BASKETBALL VS. TIME

he scores!
he shoots!

A VERY PLEASANT
MOMENT

"this slight but
definite
'secondary maximum'"

RELAX

an easy listening tune
for the crew in *Dark Star*:
"The Dust Clouds
of the Southern Milky Way"

IMPRESSIVE (I)

speaking in tongues
and holding a snake
lulled by music
is one thing
(are one thing?), but
drinking strychnine
is another

IMPRESSIVE (II)

I can't believe
I spelled "strychnine"
right without looking it up

SHOWS THROUGH

they try to teach spelling
phonetically
(you can't even spell
"phonetically" phonetically),
but studies show that good spellers
visualize the word
they want to spell

FLASH

the flashbulb
behind the eyes

HIS NAME IS AN ODE
WRITTEN BY ASTRO

O. Romer

BEGINNING OF A NOVEL
WRITTEN BY SNOOPY

on the night of
August 10, 1932,
the star began
to brighten

SCORPIUS

BOTH IN TRAINING

the first time
I saw
a scorpion,
it was on the ceiling

SERPENS CAUDA

ITS FULL GLORY REVEALED ONLY ON LONG-EXPOSURE PHOTOGRAPHS

the camera

DZIGA VERTOV

too bad his brother
didn't take the name Dzaga

TIME-ELAPSED

there's an Eagle Nebula
and two first magnitude
stars, Vega and Altair,
also considered eagles

MODERATE CAPACITY

"the more evanescent points
of more minute components"

FASCINATING DETAIL

"the most spectacular
of the diffuse"

FORMIDABLE STREAM OF
EVERY KIND OF LIGHT

Jackson Mac Low's
Complete Light Poems
is one of my favorite books

THINK OF THE SINUS
PROBLEMS

a cloud of dust and gas
36 trillion miles high

THE NIGHT SKY BY
MOSCOW MAP MAKERS

accurate distances are hard
to obtain owing to
strong obscuration

ANOTHER TYPE OF
OBSCURATION

luminosity equal to
26,000 suns

CLUSTER

simply
the densest part
of it

AND OF COURSE (I)

there's a Red Square Nebula
close by, named due to
its similarities
to the Red Rectangle Nebula

AND OF COURSE (II)

there's no Red Wedge around now

AND WHAT ISN'T

in transition between
Class 0
and Class 1

I CAN'T REMEMBER WHO SAID IT
(I)

philosophy aside, whatever
actually happens,
happens to *me*

BRIHADARANYAKA UPANISAD
1.4.6

Food and eater—that
is the extent
of this whole world

or

so much is this whole
universe, either food
or the eater of food

BUT

"Offer your body, organs,
viscera, etc., to root
and lineage lamas, yidam
deities, wisdom dharma
protectors and guardians,
shidaks, nagas, the hundred
thousand action dakinis,
the King of the upper devils,
the Queen of the lower
devils, gyalpo, senmo, t'eu,
nyen types, tsen spirits. . . ."

I CAN'T REMEMBER WHO
SAID IT (II)

no self, OK, but no memory—
that can be a problem:
I don't know where the
previous section came from

WALT WHITMAN,
SONG OF MYSELF,
SECTION 1

"every atom belonging to me
as good belongs to you"

BUT

I wrote this, and the views
and opinions expressed herein
are those of the individual writer
and do not necessarily represent
the views and opinions
of any corporation
or any of its respective
affiliates or employees

TWISTY THOUGHT

yesterday or tomorrow,
this piece may have been
completely different

T. J. CLARK ON POUSSIN'S SNAKE AGAIN

the snake "is above all
a body that can constantly
recreate its own form,
and seems to have no 'given'
or optimum disposition
of its parts in space"
(*The Sight of Death* 179)

ANOTHER TWISTY THOUGHT

in curved space,
inspection = circumspection

IN CURVED SPACE

a straight line
is not
the shortest distance
between two points

A LOGOS

alogos

LYRA

FIRST, OTHER THAN

Lyra was the first
constellation I found
when I started looking for them
(I already knew
the Big Dipper)

PHOTOGRAPH

Lyra was the first
star other than
the sun
to be photographed

ANOTHER WAY I'M NOT LIKE WALT WHITMAN

I don't like
having my
photograph taken

TAKEN

and a photograph is
always *taken*—it removes
information from you (and makes it
obsolete, too)

AND

I've been feeling
a bit tired lately

AND

that's another reason
why mosquito
bites are evil

LIGHT ON THE SUBJECT

that's a subjective
(relative) view

SPECTRUM

Vega is also the first star
to have a photograph
of its spectrum taken

AND NOW

it's electromagnetic
spectrum
is rather flat

X-RAY

Vega was the first main-sequence
star beyond our solar system's
sun shown to be
an emitter of X-rays

WHAT BIG TEETH YOU HAVE

dental X-rays
have been linked with cancer

INFORMATION LOSS (I)

and now Lyra is not
listed in *Burnham's
Celestial Handbook*

MISTAKE

wait—I'm looking
under Vega: Lyra's
there, in Volume II

INFORMATION LOSS (II)

Carlo Rovelli says that
ignorance
is missing information—
which I think
in Rovelli's context
means "undiscovered"

ROVELLI AGAIN

if we have "a *complete*
description of a system,
all the variables of the
system are on the same
footing; none of them
act as a time variable"
and thus time is not
a factor: but, since
we "never see a single
elementary particle or
a single quantum of space,"
our experience is of
macroscopic averages of
microscopic events,
and averages
"disperse heat
and, intrinsically,
generate time"
(*Reality is Not What It Seems*
252)

THE WAY THAT CAN BE NAMED IS NOT THE ETERNAL WAY

Daniil Kharms noted that,
since the way to live longer
depends on self-denial,
the way to become immortal
is to always do that
which you don't want
to do: so maybe another
way to live forever is

always to not know,
to neither give nor
receive information

JUST DON'T DO IT

don't quote me
on that

WORN OUT

to do nothing is tiring

ELEMENTARY

a "complete system" sounds
to me to be a *completed*
system: a stasis:
for me (a microsystem)
to know only a part
(another microsystem)—
not a whole, not nothing—
creates time, gives me time

SAND

"To see a World in a Grain of Sand
And a Heaven in a Wild Flower
Hold Infinity in the palm of your
      hand
and Eternity in an hour"—no thanks

BEWARE (I)

of people who
"have so much
to offer"

BEWARE (II)

especially if that
description
is offered by
the person him- or herself

SUSPICIONS CONFIRMED

"had earned a Master's
degree in guidance
counseling from Xavier
University in Cincinnati
and an Associate's degree
in mortuary science
from the Cincinnati College
of Mortuary Science"
(C S Giscombe,
Ohio Railroads 34)

THEY WERE RIPE FOR
THE TAKING

the Boorong, indigenous
people of Northwestern
Victoria, named
Vega "the flying Loan"

JOYCE

silence, cunning, and exile

MIGHT BE GOOD, MIGHT BE BAD

a loose translation
meaning "falling" or "landing"

FALLING OR LANDING

the pole star
around 12,000 BCE
and the pole star
around 14,000 CE

IN BETWEEN

Harpo's harp solo
is always a good time
to get popcorn
or find the bathroom

ROVELLI

"Carlo Rovelli" sounds like
a name one of Chico's
characters would have

A LITTLE INFORMATION,
SORRY

"Chico" is pronounced
"Chick-o,"
not "Cheek-o"

PERCENT

the percentage of those
who see the start of
a Harpo solo vs. those
those who watch
the whole thing
must be low, especially
compared to those
who see the beginning of
a shoot-out vs. those who
watch through to the end

BUT

not everyone makes it
to the end of a shoot-out

MINUTES GONE FROM
YOUR LIFE

but maybe the Harpo
situation changed
with VHS tapes,
since you could stop
those anytime

you needed a break
and didn't have to wait
for a slower moment

LATER BUT NOT NECESSARILY
THE END

Suicide (Alan Vega
and Martin Rev)
were the last of
the New York 70s/80s
bands that I came to like

SUICIDE

when My Bloody Valentine
(not a NY band, I realize)
sang the chorus to
"Sue is Fine," we
were pretty sure they
were singing "Su-i-cide,"
but we couldn't be sure

FINE

"fine" is a rote response
when you're really
depressed, and someone
who is a stranger or
only an acquaintance
asks how you're doing

SILENCE

Harpo had trouble
memorizing dialog

NOT IMMORTAL, BUT 68
YEARS

Harpo could speak, but
he never says a word
onscreen

MISTAKE (I)

Harpo died
at age 75

MISTAKE (II)

Harpo's harp
was tuned incorrectly

Also by Mark Cunningham

bl(A)nk. Independently published. (2023).
morfact. Independently published. (2023).
sort/quantum. Independently published. (2023).
A Longer Life. Text with video by Dale Wisely. (2022). YouTube. <https://youtu.be/cSWPjndC7fM>.
Future Words. if p then q. (2020).
"f(l)ights." *Otoliths* 56 (Southern Summer 2020). A 110-piece sequence. <www.the-otolith.blogspot.com/2020/01/mark-cunningham.html>.
"Fail Lure." *Otoliths* 52 (Southern Summer 2019). An 81-piece sequence. <www.the-otolith.blogspot.com/2018/11/mark-cunningham.html>.
multizon(e). Text with video by Dale Wisely. Right Hand Pointing. (2019). <www.issues.righthandpointing.net/multizone>.
Alphabetical Basho. Beard of Bees. (2016). <www.beardofbees.com/pubs/Alphabetical_Basho.pdf>.

And Suddenly It's Evening. Beard of Bees. (2014). <www.beardofbees.com/pubs/And_Suddenly_Its_Evening.pdf>.

Regularly Scheduled. Beard of Bees. (2012). <www.beardofbees.com/pubs/Regularly_Scheduled.pdf>.

Scissors and Starfish. Right Hand Pointing. (2012).

Helicotremors. Otoliths. (2012).

specimens. BlazeVOX. (2011).

nightlightnight. With photographs by Mel Nichols. Right Hand Pointing. (2009). <www.archives.righthandpointing.com/nightlightnight>.

71 Leaves. BlazeVOX. (2008). <www.blazevox.org/ebk-mCunningham%20REAL.pdf>.

80 Beetles. Otoliths. (2008).

Body Language. Tarpaulin Sky Press. (2008).

www.ingramcontent.com/pod-product-compliance
Lightning Source LLC
Chambersburg PA
CBHW051654040426
42446CB00009B/1135